A

A Prairie Alphabet

B

TEXT BY JO BANNATYNE – CUGNET
ART BY YVETTE MOORE

TUNDRA BOOKS

C

A Prairie Alphabet

When the early French explorers first saw the North American plains they described it as a vast treeless landscape — "a sea of grass." They called it *prairie* which is the French word for "meadow."

The prairies extend approximately 5,000 kilometers (over 3,000 miles) between northern Alberta almost to the Gulf of Mexico. In Canada, it includes the southern part of the provinces of Alberta, Saskatchewan and Manitoba. In the United States, it includes the Dakotas, Nebraska, Kansas, Oklahoma and parts of Montana, Iowa, Minnesota, Wisconsin, Illinois, Missouri and Texas.

On the prairies we have extremes in climate — hot dry summers and cold snowy winters. Summertime temperatures can reach over 40 degrees Celsius (104°F) and winter temperatures can drop to below -40 degrees Celsius (-40°F).

The first settlers were lured to the prairies by the rich, fertile soils and the promise of free land. The labors of the pioneers soon transformed the "sea of grass" into acres of wheat, and the region was referred to as "the breadbasket of the world."

Today, agriculture still dominates the prairies and our way of life. The land is a pattern of farms and ranches, larger than those of the past, interspersed by towns and cities.

Some people say there's not much to see on the prairies but we say we have more time to see it. This book will afford you the opportunity to see the real beauty of the prairies. Here are the prairies through the eyes of children.

Dedicated to the children of the prairies.
Y.M.
J.B.C.

We auction our Aberdeen Angus at Agribition.

a

Our Belgians, Bill and Bob, bed in the barn.

C

Craig sees a combine clearing a crop of canola.

D Dan discovers deer drinking at the dugout at dawn. d

E   The engine pulls empty cars up to the elevators.

F   **Our family grows food to feed families far away.**

Gophers gaze at geese flying over the grassland.

H It's hard work hauling hay to the Herefords. h

I   Autumn finds icicles on the irrigation sprinkler.   i

J   The judges gave Jesse's jar of jam first prize.   j

K My kite kicks. I knot the string around my knuckles. k

L | Livestock line up to come in as lightning flashes. | l

M   A mouse munches a meal of millet by moonlight.

N   When we need neighbors, they are always near.   n

 Oil pumps stand out like over-sized grasshoppers.

 The prairie has the pattern of a patchwork quilt.

 Q   The quarter horses stand quietly by the quonset.   q

R   We root from our ringside seats at the rodeo.   r

S

Sarah shivered when she saw sundogs in the sky.

S

T | Teresa takes her toolbox and thermos to the tractor. |

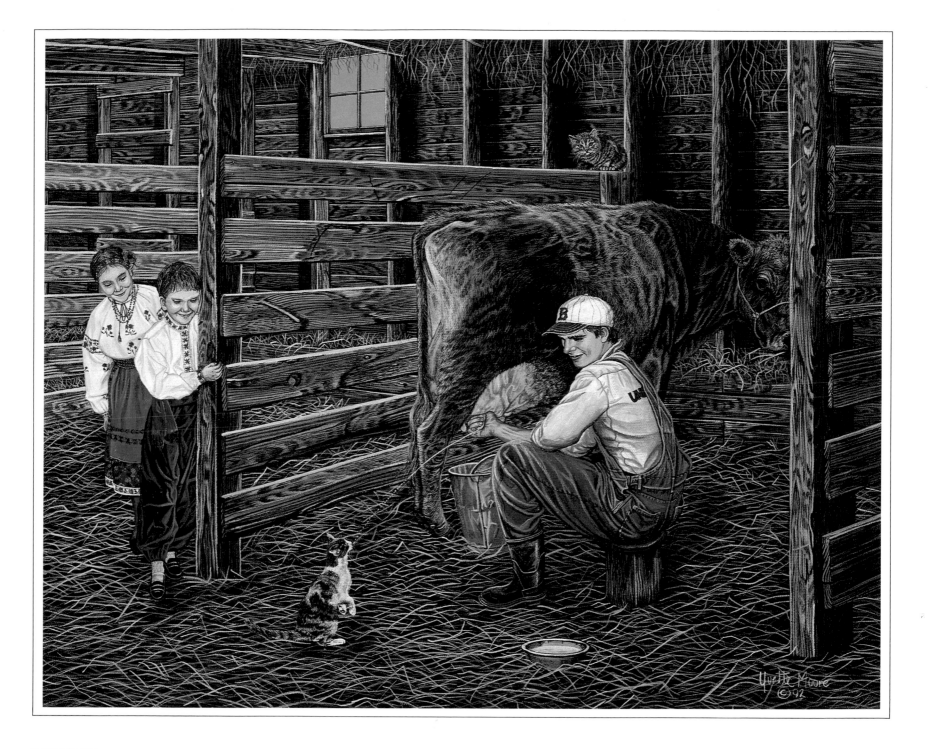

U   Uncle pulls up and down on the udder to get milk.   u

 The vet came in his van to vaccinate the calves.

W   We wade through the wheat waving in the wind.

 At the X sign be extra careful to look both ways.

We trade yarns and yawns by the yellow yardlight.

Z   At zero degrees we cover the zinnias and zucchini.   Z

Aa adolescent, adult, advertisements (ads), audience, aisle, animal, arena, arm, asters, auctioneer, audio equipment

Bb bale, barn cat, barrel, beams, bell, billygoat, birds, bit, blocks, blue jeans, boards, boat (stone boat), bolts, boys, boots, box, bottle, bridle, broom, brothers, bucket, bulb

Cc calf, cans (Coke), cap, cattails, cheeks, child, church or chapel, city, clothes, clover (yellow), clouds, collie, COOP (capitals on cap), coveralls, countryside, cow, crow, culvert

Dd dairy cows, daisy, dandelion, dirt, discer, ditch, dock, doe, ducks

Ee elbow, electricity pole, engineer, evergreens, exit, Eyebrow

Ff fabric (quilt), faces, fall, father, feet, female, fence, fields, fingers, flax (blue field), flowers, fly, fork, friends, frying pan, (note the hats—Flexicoil, 4-H, Focus, etc.)

Gg gander, garden, garter snake, grill gate (Texas gate), girls, glasses (field), gold, goldenrod, gourd, graded road (also known as grid road), granaries, grass, gravel, green

Hh hair, hammer, hands, hay fork, hayrack, handle, head, heel, heifer, hens, herd, hide, horseshoe, 4-H

Ii ice, imprint, infant, International truck

Jj jars, jack-o'-lantern (pumpkins), jean jumper, jelly, jug, juice, Junior class, junk

Kk kerchief, kid, kildeer, knapsack, knee, kochia

Ll lake, lamb, land, lariat, leaves, Leghorn rooster, legs, license plate, logs, lumber

Mm mark (foot mark), mice, milk can, moon, mouser, mouth, mud

Nn napkins, nasturtiums, nail, needlepoint, nest, newborn, newspaper, name — New Norway, numbers — nineteen nineteen (1919)

Oo oats, oil rig, oil pump, orange (on pump jack), outdoors, overalls, owl

Pp pane, parallel fields, pasture, path, people, pickup truck, pilot, plane, pond, ponies, posts

Qq quack grass, quartet of quackers!, quill

Rr rain slicker, rear, red, rider, riggin, ring, roost

Ss sapling, scarf, seat, shade, shadows, sheds, shelterbelt, shield (windshield), shinny, shoulder, shrubs, silo, skis, sky, slacks, sleeves, sleigh, slope, slough, snow, snowdrifts, snowmobile, spruce, stem, sticks (hockey), stubble, summer fallow, sun

Tt tank, tailgate (truck), teenager, temple, thumb, tires, tom (turkey), tracks, trailer, trash bin, trees, tricycle, truck, turkeys

Uu Ukrainian clothing, university (shirt), upholstery, upstairs

Vv vaccine, Valleyview, vane, vest, vial, visitors, vitamins

Ww wagon, wheel, wind, windmill, window, wire (fence), wood buildings

Xx X-sign, x's in the crossbars on the barn. That's all we found. Can you find more?

Yy yard, Yorkshire hogs, Yvette's signature in the corner, a 'Y' in the gravel road

Zz zebra plant, a zigzag pattern on the fence, zip code, zippers

A Agribition is a week-long international agriculture trade fair held every November in Regina, Saskatchewan. People come from all over the world to see the best in livestock and produce. Thousands of schoolchildren, rural and urban, tour through the barns and exhibits. Agribition is an opportunity to teach them more about agriculture. Auctions are especially exciting, but my advice is to sit on your hands. At one auction two dozen eggs sold for $8,000!

B Boys are breaking in a young Belgian with a stone boat. Pioneers used stone boats for transporting stones and other heavy objects on the farm. Heavy horse teams have been known to pull loads of over 10,000 pounds. The bay-colored Belgians are my favorite.

C During harvest you see combines out in the fields, chugging and grinding away as they thresh the crop, separating the seeds from the stalks. Big grain trucks haul the grain from the combine to storage bins or the grain elevator. With all this working machinery it is not a safe place for children. The child in the picture is busy with a harvest of his own — picking cans in the ditch which he will take to a recycling station and collect five cents per can.

D Dugouts are the most common method of water storage on prairie farms. These man-made ponds are usually at least 14 feet deep and are located to collect runoff from spring thaw (melting snow) and rainfall. We have several dugouts — one for our home use and several for our livestock needs. Some farmers stock their dugouts with fish and create their own fishing hole.

E Grain elevators were the first prairie skyscrapers. Sometimes referred to as "prairie giants," they stand out clearly against the flat landscape. You can see them from great distances. Farmers haul grain to the elevator by truck. Here it is weighed, graded, cleaned and stored until it is loaded into railway cars. The engineer will pull the loaded grain cars all the way to a seaport terminal where the grain will be transferred onto oceangoing ships.

F For children, the best part about harvest is meals in the field. Everyone is in a hurry to get the crop off so we eat in the field to save time. Because we are working hard, the food seems to taste even better than usual. It becomes a big family picnic. I wonder if the wheat we took off this field will become Italian pasta or may be used to make bread in Korea.

G Who can ignore the loud honking overhead? It's easy to identify them as Canada geese. See the large brownish-gray body and the black head and neck with the bold white cheek patch? They are migrating south to warmer climes. A sure sign that winter is just around the corner. You gophers better get busy and dig your tunnel a little deeper if you want to stay warm.

H Herefords are one of the most common breed of cattle on the prairie because they perform well despite a changing climate. When the pastures are covered with snow, we feed out hay baled earlier in the summer. The hay bales are heavy but everyone pitches in to get the job done!

I Farmers who have access to a large water supply such as ground wells or a lake use irrigation to increase crop yields. There are different systems of irrigation. The one pictured is called a wheelmove or sideroll system. The first autumn frost has transformed this field into a crop of icicles!

J Prairie folk like to grow food and take great pride in their gardening skills. Usually there's more than we can eat. By autumn the cold room shelves are full. Jesse has learned home preserving skills by working at her mother's side. She is very proud her efforts won the first prize at the local fair.

K It's a rare day on the prairies that you can't fly a kite. The wind always seems present. Is that because there's nothing to stop it? Children grow up enjoying the wide open spaces and find ways of entertaining themselves. Only the shrill cry of a kildeer interrupts this peaceful scene.

L Livestock is another word for farm animals. Here we see cows, chickens, sheep and a horse anxious to get inside away from the oncoming storm. On the prairies we seem to get our best lightning storms after a real hot spell. I enjoy watching these summer fireworks — from inside the house!

M Every farm has a mouse or two. Mice are nocturnal, so every night they come out looking for food. There are always bits of grain to be found — like this farmer's millet. Life would be pretty easy for mice if farmers didn't keep barn cats.

N Neighbors are quick to respond if someone needs help. Once our neighbor was in a car accident and was unable to harvest his crop. Neighbors came, leaving their crops in the field to harvest his first. Here a young mother whose leg has been hurt happily greets the arrival of home-cooked meals. The rural community is closely knit although homes are separated by great distances.

O Once the prairies were covered by lush vegetation like a tropical jungle and dinosaurs were king. Now beneath the cactus and ploughed fields we find fossil remains and deeper down, the precious by-product of the past, oil.

P The Snowbirds are Canada's precision military aerobatic team based out of Canadian Forces Base Moose Jaw. Who gets a better view of the prairies than these pilots? Watching the team perform is like watching a ballet in the air. See how tight their formation is? There are five planes in this picture. Can you find them?

Q A quonset is a corrugated steel building shaped like a half-moon. The straight side forms the floor. First built by the military in World War II, farm boys who served in the army were quick to see the possibilities for these buildings and brought the idea home. Quonsets are used for storing machinery. They are fast and easy to erect, require little upkeep, and their shape is well suited to climate demands, letting wind sweep over them and shedding rain and snow.

R The Calgary Exhibition and Stampede is a world-famous rodeo and agriculture fair held every July in Calgary, Alberta. Rodeo competitions include the traditional tests of cowboy skills – riding, roping and racing. There's steer wrestling, calf roping, bronco busting and the always exciting chuckwagon races. For cowboys aged 10 to 14 years, the Boys' Steer Riding Championship is a great attraction. This young man is having the ride of his life.

S Sundogs are bright circular spots near the sun that seem to form a solar halo. They occur on the prairies when ice crystals are suspended in the air and it is extremely dry. Gramma says when you see sundogs, colder weather is on its way.

T Tractors are today's work horse, the most versatile machinery on a farm. They pull wagons, cultivators, discers, balers and rock pickers; they power other machinery such as augers, mixmills and snow blowers; they run in any kind of weather and at any time of the day, and at the end of a day's work the tractor needs only to be parked, not fed and bedded down in the barn like a horse.

U Chores must be done before young people go out in the evening. The cow must be milked and the eggs must be picked. Two children are already dressed in their Ukrainian dance costume for tonight's multicultural event. I think I can hear their mother: "Now don't you children get dirty. Stay out of the barn."

V The veterinarian is an animal doctor who helps farmers and ranchers ensure the health of their livestock. In the spring, new calves are rounded up and vaccinated to protect them from disease. Some calves are more cooperative than others so the vet often needs help.

W Wheat is the most important cereal in the world and is the chief crop grown on the prairies. The flour from this grain is used to make such staples in our diet as bread and pasta. Just before harvest the prairies do seem to be an endless golden sea of wheat.

X Children who live in rural areas go to school on a school bus. Many spend over an hour a day traveling. It gets pretty boring after a while following the same route but you sure know what's going on in the neighborhood. The law states that buses must stop at railroad tracks. It's everyone's job to look both ways for trains.

Y As darkness descends the yardlight illuminates the farmyard. It makes it so much easier to check the livestock and do our night chores. And traveling home late at night from the city we use the shining yardlights that dot the prairie to landmark our way, just as sailors at sea use the stars to chart their course. It is always reassuring to see yardlights because we know there's a place to go if we need help.

Z Prairie people are weather watchers because with agriculture our fortunes are very much tied to the land and the weather. The climate is very dynamic, always changing, so we listen to weather forecasts and watch the thermometer. As the temperature drops to the freezing point, we know it means crop damage. At least we can save the garden from frost by covering it with blankets.

This is the prairies today in an alphabet book for children and an art book for adults.

An enormous success when first published, *A Prairie Alphabet* went through five printings in its first year and inspired *A Prairie Alphabet Musical Parade*, a symphony for children composed by Elizabeth Raum and performed by the Regina Symphony Orchestra. It won the Mr. Christie's Book Award for illustration, one of Canada's leading awards, and was a finalist for the Ruth Schwartz Award, the Saskatchewan Book of the Year Award, the Amelia Frances Howard-Gibbon Award, and earned a Certificate of Merit from New York's Art Directors Club.

Writer Jo Bannatyne-Cugnet and artist Yvette Moore were born on the prairies, grew up there and stayed on to raise families. Each is the mother of four. What they have given us is the prairies as seen through their children's eyes, thereby making it fresh for all of us.

Yvette Moore's art has been classified as magic realism. It is apt, because her paintings reveal the most magic when they are most realistic. The smallness of children, animals and objects is set against the vastness of land and sky. Children wade waist-high through miles of waving grain. Gophers watch geese flying above a road forever. An oilpump looks like a grasshopper on a distant hill. Her art has made her one of the prairies' most popular artists in recent years and her paintings and prints are exhibited in many western art galleries. She lives in Moose Jaw, Saskatchewan.

Jo Bannatyne-Cugnet worked closely with artist Moore to develop this multifaceted work. Although each painting is a work of art in itself, it is also a puzzle. Alliterative captions sum up each scene and children are encouraged to search out additional objects beginning with the same letter. In recent years Jo has added writing to her several careers. After graduating with a degree in nursing from the University of Saskatchewan, she married a farmer and moved to a farm outside of Weyburn, Saskatchewan, where she still lives.

Copyright © 1992 Jo Bannatyne-Cugnet: text
Copyright © 1992 Yvette Moore: art

Published in Canada by Tundra Books, *McClelland & Stewart Young Readers*, 481 University Avenue, Toronto, Ontario M5G 2E9

Published in the United States by Tundra Books of Northern New York, P.O. Box 1030, Plattsburgh, New York 12901

Library of Congress Catalog Number: 92-80414

Design by Dan O'Leary

Transparencies by Jim Shipley

Canadian Cataloguing in Publication Data

Bannatyne-Cugnet, Jo
   A prairie alphabet

ISBN 0-88776-292-1 (bound)   ISBN 0-88776-323-5 (pbk.)

1. English language – Alphabet – Juvenile literature.   2. Farm life – Prairie Provinces – Juvenile literature.   3. Prairie Provinces – Pictorial works. I. Moore, Yvette.   II. Title.

PEll55.B35   1998   j421'.1   C98-932438-9

We acknowledge the support of the Canada Council for the Arts for our publishing program.

We acknowledge the financial support of the Government of Canada through the Book Publishing Industry Development Program for our publishing activities.

The cover reproduction of the Mr. Christie Book Award® Seal is used with the permission of Nabisco Brands Ltd. Toronto, Ontario, Canada.©

Printed and bound in Canada

11 12 13 14 15   04 03 02 01 00